CYBER SECURITY
AWARENESS

EMPLOYEE EDITION 2023

PAUL M. CARR

Contents

Introduction to the Book

In today's digital age, cyber security has become a critical concern for organisations of all sizes. With the increasing prevalence of cyber-attacks and data breaches, it has become imperative for companies to educate their employees on the best practices of cyber security awareness. Employees can unknowingly create vulnerabilities that leave their organisation open to cyber-attacks. Therefore, ensuring that all employees have the necessary knowledge and skills to protect the organisation's data and assets is essential.

This book on cyber security awareness for employees aims to provide a comprehensive guide to help employees understand the importance of cyber security and develop the necessary skills to protect themselves and their organisation from cyber threats. It covers various topics, including common types of cyber-attacks, ways to identify and prevent phishing attacks, ransomware, and social engineering. While also providing information and guidance on best practices involving Password Management, Two-Factor-Authentication, Remote Working, Mobile Devices, VPNs, Removable Media, and more. At the end of each section, there is a brief on current stats on how the chosen topic impacts the real world, stats are a collection of data from the world wide web.

By the end of this book, you'll have a deeper understanding of your organisation's main threats and the best practices to protect against them. You'll also be equipped with the necessary knowledge and skills to become a more vigilant and proactive employee, helping to keep your organisation safe from cyber-attacks.

Introduction to the Author

Hello, and thank you for choosing my book. My name is Paul Carr, and I am the author of this book on Cyber Security Awareness – Employee Edition 2023. As someone who has always been passionate about Cyber Security, I am thrilled to be able to share my knowledge and insights with you.

Over the past decade, I have developed a deep understanding of Cyber Security, which has been shaped by my working professional experiences in vulnerability management, penetration testing, ethical hacking, and security research. I started as an intern and moved up the ranks to a senior executive in the cyber division of one of the world's largest organisations, to where I am today as a very happy manager of product security for an amazing software-as-a-service company. I am also the founder of my own business based on providing cyber security awareness called **Cyber Onboarding.** I also have a degree in Computer Security and Digital Forensics. Through this book, I hope to provide readers with a comprehensive guide to security awareness and to help them gain a deeper understanding of what to be aware of in the realm of cyber security.

Thank you for taking the time to read this book, and I hope that you find it informative and helps you and your organisation stay safe.

CHAPTER ONE

PASSWORD MANAGEMENT

Passwords are the first line of defence against unauthorised access to your company's digital assets. Strong passwords can protect sensitive information from cybercriminals, while weak passwords can leave your business vulnerable to attacks. Therefore, employees need to understand how to create and maintain strong passwords to protect themselves and their organisation.

Here are some tips on how to create and maintain strong passwords:

- **Use a strong and unique password**

  A strong password is at **least 12 characters long** and includes a combination of:

    - Upper case letters, e.g. A, B, C, D...
    - Lowercase letters, e.g., a, b, c, d...
    - Numbers, e.g., 1, 2, 3, 4...
    - Special characters, e.g. ~, [, ?, *...

- **Don't share your passwords**

  Never share your password with anyone, including your colleagues or the IT department. In the event your IT department asks for your password, work with them to carry out the exchange in a secure manner.

- **Change your passwords regularly**

  Change your passwords at least every 90 days, or as per company policy, or immediately if you suspect it has been disclosed to anyone. This will reduce the risk of your password being compromised and will ensure that you are using a new and secure password.

- **Don't reuse passwords**

  Don't use the same password for multiple accounts, as this makes it easier for hackers to access your accounts if they compromise just one password. After an attacker gets your password, they will then try all the leading accounts, such as:

- Travelling websites
- Online banking
- Social media platforms
- Payroll
- Insurance sites
- CRM
- Email Facilities

- Use multi-factor authentication

  Multi-factor authentication (MFA) adds an extra layer of security to your accounts by requiring a second factor, such as a fingerprint or a code sent to your phone, in addition to your password. Enable MFA wherever possible.

- Avoid using personal information

  Avoid using personal information such as your name, date of birth, or address in your passwords. This information is easily accessible to hackers and can be used to guess your password.

Stats on bad password management.

- The most commonly used password is "123456", followed by "password". (Source: NordPass 2021 Report)
- 81% of data breaches are due to weak, reused, or stolen passwords. (Source: Verizon 2021 Data Breach Investigations Report)
- A password of just six lowercase letters can be cracked in under 10 minutes. (Source: CyberNews)

- The average user has 100 passwords, but only 20% of users have unique passwords for each account. (Source: NordPass 2021 Report)
- Brute-force attacks, in which an attacker uses automated software to try a large number of password combinations, can crack an eight-character password in just a few hours. (Source: CyberNews)
- In 2020, over 5 billion records were exposed in data breaches, with the majority of these records being usernames and passwords. (Source: RiskBased 2020 Year-End Data Breach QuickView Report)
- The cost of a data breach caused by a stolen or weak password is estimated to be €139/$148 per record. (Source: IBM 2020 Cost of a Data Breach Report)

Final thoughts on password security

Creating and maintaining strong passwords is crucial for protecting you and your company's digital assets. Each employee should understand how to create and maintain a secure password to reduce the risk of cyber-attacks.

CHAPTER TWO

VPNS

In today's increasingly connected world, the use of VPNs has become an essential part of maintaining the security and privacy of online communication. VPNs, or virtual private networks, are tools that allow users to securely connect to the internet, protecting their data and online activities from prying eyes. In the context of security awareness for employees, VPNs can be a valuable tool in protecting company data and preventing cyber threats.

What is a VPN?

A VPN, or virtual private network, works by creating a secure and private connection between a user's device and a remote server. When a user connects to a VPN, their internet traffic is encrypted and sent through the remote server, making it more difficult for others to see their online activities. This can help protect their data and privacy, as well as allow them to access content that may be restricted in their location.

Why are VPNs important to me and my organisation?

As more employees work remotely and rely on internet-based communication tools, the risk of cyber-attacks and data breaches has increased. To protect company data and prevent unauthorised access, employees need to use secure methods of accessing the internet. VPNs can provide an additional layer of security to protect sensitive data and prevent cyber-attacks.

For example, when employees connect to public Wi-Fi networks, they are at risk of having their data intercepted by hackers. Public Wi-Fi networks are often unsecured, meaning that anyone can access them without a password. This makes them an easy target for cybercriminals looking to steal sensitive data such as login credentials and financial information. By using a VPN, employees can protect their internet traffic from prying eyes, making it more difficult for hackers to intercept their data.

Similarly, when employees travel or work from remote locations, they may be accessing the internet from unfamiliar networks. These networks may be less secure than the company's network, making them vulnerable to cyber-attacks. By using a VPN, employees can ensure that their internet connection is secure, regardless of the network they are using.

CHAPTER THREE

TWO-FACTOR-AUTHENTICATION

Two-factor authentication (2FA) is a security process in which a user provides two different authentication factors to verify their identity. With the increasing threat of cyber-attacks, 2FA has become an essential security measure for businesses to protect their sensitive information and data from unauthorised access.

There are multiple different names for 2FA, some of the most common are:

- Multi-Factor-Authentication (MFA)
- Two-Step Verification
- Dual-Factor Authentication

As an employee, it's crucial to understand the importance of 2FA and the role it plays in securing your company's information.

Why is 2FA essential?

Passwords are no longer enough to protect your accounts and sensitive information. Cybercriminals can easily guess or obtain passwords through phishing attacks or data breaches. Once they have access to your password, they can potentially access all your accounts and data, putting your company at risk.

By using 2FA, you add an extra layer of protection to your accounts, making it more challenging for cybercriminals to access them. Even if they have your password, they would need the second authentication factor, which only you possess, to access your account.

How does 2FA work?

2FA works by combining three different authentication factors:

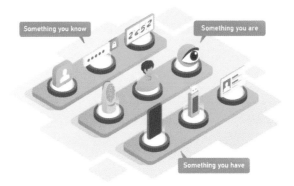

- Something you know

  This could be your password, a PIN, or the answer to a security question. This is something you know that's unique to you.

- Something you have

  This could be your smartphone, a security token, or a smart card. This is something physical that only you possess.

- **Something you are**

  This could be facial recognition, fingerprint or a retina scanner. This is something within your body.

When you log in to an account with 2FA enabled, you'll need to provide two of the above authentication factors to access your account. For example, after entering your password, you may receive a text message or a push notification on your smartphone asking you to confirm your identity. Only after you've provided both factors will you be granted access to your account.

Best practices for using 2FA:

- **Use it on all your accounts**

  Wherever possible, enable 2FA on all your accounts, especially those containing sensitive information like banking or financial data, personal or work email, and social media.

- **Choose a strong password**

  Your password should be unique, complex, and not easily guessable. Avoid using simple passwords or common phrases that can be easily cracked.

- **Use an authenticator app**

  Instead of relying on SMS or email-based 2FA, use an authenticator app like Google Authenticator, Authy, or Microsoft Authenticator. These apps generate one-time codes that expire after a short period, making them more secure than SMS or email-based 2FA.

- Store your backup codes safely

    Many services provide backup codes that you can use to access your account if you don't have access to your 2FA device. Make sure to store these backup codes safely, preferably in a password manager or a physical safe.

Stats on using 2FA

- In 2020, 92% of organisations surveyed by Microsoft reported that they use 2FA for at least one application. (Source: Microsoft Security)
- Google found that enabling 2FA can block 100% of automated bots, 99% of bulk phishing attacks, and 66% of targeted attacks. (Source: Google)
- The use of 2FA can reduce the risk of account takeover by 99.9%. (Source: Google)
- In a survey of 2,000 adults, 66% said they use 2FA to secure their accounts. (Source: LastPass)
- 2FA can also help to comply with regulations such as the General Data Protection Regulation (GDPR) and the Health Insurance Portability and Accountability Act (HIPAA). (Source: Duo Security)

Final thoughts on 2FA

2FA is a crucial security measure that adds an extra layer of protection to your accounts and sensitive information. As an employee, it's essential to understand its importance and follow best practices when using it. By doing so, you'll help keep your company's information and data safe from cybercriminals.

CHAPTER FOUR

REMOVABLE MEDIA

As an employee, you may be tempted to use various removable media devices such as USB drives, external hard drives, SD cards, and others, to store and transfer data between computers or to work from home. While removable media devices are convenient, they also pose significant security risks that could compromise sensitive information or your employer's network.

In this section, we will discuss cyber security with removable media for employees and provide tips on how to use these devices safely and securely.

- **Malware/Viruses**

  One of the primary risks of using removable media devices is that they can carry viruses and malware that can infect your computer or your organisation's network. These malicious programs can steal sensitive data, damage systems, or cause disruptions to normal operations.

- **Lost or stolen**

  Another risk is that removable media devices can be lost or stolen, potentially exposing sensitive information to unauthorised individuals. For example, if you store your company's financial data or customer information on a USB drive, and it falls into the wrong hands, the consequences could be severe.

- **Use encrypted devices**

  To protect sensitive data on removable media devices, consider using encrypted devices. Encryption scrambles the data on the device, making it unreadable without a decryption key. This makes it difficult for attackers to access your data even if the device falls into the wrong hands.

- **Use secure transfer methods**

  When transferring data from a removable media device, make sure you use secure transfer methods such as encrypted email or secure file transfer protocols. Avoid using unsecured methods like regular email or file-sharing services, as they are vulnerable to interception and compromise.

- Scan devices for viruses

  Before using a removable media device, scan it for viruses and malware using antivirus software. If you detect any threats, do not use the device and notify your IT department.

- Keep devices with you

  When carrying removable media devices, keep them with you at all times or lock them in a secure place. Never leave them unattended in public places or in your car, as they can be stolen easily.

- Not for personal use

  Avoid using removable media devices for personal use, as they may not have the same security measures as your work devices.

- Report incidents

  If you suspect that a removable media device has been lost or stolen or that it has been compromised in any way, report it immediately to your IT department or security team. They can take steps to mitigate the risks and prevent further damage.

Stats on Removable Media and Security

- In a survey of 300 IT professionals, 83% said that their organisation had experienced a data breach caused by an external device, such as a USB drive. (Source: Apricorn)

- 62% of respondents to a survey by Veritas said that their organisation had experienced a data breach or data loss due to the use of removable media. (Source: Veritas)
- In the same Veritas survey, 54% of respondents said that their organisation did not have a policy for the use of removable media. (Source: Veritas)
- A study by the University of Illinois found that 48% of people who found a USB drive in a public place inserted it into their computer. (Source: University of Illinois)
- In 2019, the US Department of Defence banned the use of removable media due to the risks of data breaches and malware infections. (Source: ZDNet)

Final thoughts on Removable Media

Removable media devices are a useful tool for employees, but they also pose significant security risks. By embracing cyber security, you can protect yourself and your organisation from potential threats. Remember, cyber security is everyone's responsibility, and we all have a role to play in keeping our data and systems secure.

CHAPTER FIVE

RANSOMWARE

Ransomware is malicious software that encrypts files on a victim's computer, making them inaccessible until a ransom is paid to the attacker. It has become one of the most prevalent types of cyber-attacks in recent years, and employees are often the first line of defence against it. Therefore, employees need to be aware of the risks and take precautions to prevent ransomware attacks. Here we will discuss the basics of ransomware and provide tips for employees to prevent and respond to such attacks.

What is Ransomware?

Ransomware is a type of malware that infects a victim's computer and encrypts files to make them inaccessible. Attackers then demand payment in exchange for a decryption key that can unlock the files. The payment is usually in the form of cryptocurrency, making it difficult to trace.

Ransomware attacks can have devastating consequences for businesses, including financial loss, damage to reputation, and disruption of operations. The attackers may also steal sensitive data before encrypting the files, leading to data breaches and regulatory compliance violations.

How to Prevent Ransomware Attacks?

Preventing ransomware attacks requires a combination of technical and non-technical measures. Here are some tips for employees to prevent ransomware attacks:

- Keep software and operating systems up to date

  Attackers often exploit vulnerabilities in outdated software and operating systems to infect a computer with ransomware. Keeping software up to date with the latest security patches can prevent such attacks.

- Use strong passwords and multi-factor authentication

  Strong passwords and multi-factor authentication can make it difficult for attackers to gain access to a victim's computer or account.

- Be cautious of suspicious emails and links

  Ransomware often spreads through phishing emails and malicious links. Employees should be cautious of unsolicited emails, especially those with attachments or links.

- Back up important files regularly

  Regular backups can help mitigate the damage of a ransomware attack. If files are backed up, they can be restored without paying the ransom.

- Use anti-virus and anti-malware software

  Anti-virus and anti-malware software can detect and prevent ransomware attacks. Employees should ensure that such software is installed and up to date.

What to do in Case of Ransomware Attack?

In case of a ransomware attack, employees should take the following steps:

1. Disconnect from the network

   If it is safe to do so, disconnecting from the network can prevent the ransomware from spreading to other computers.

2. Contact IT support or the security team

   Employees should contact their IT support or security team immediately and follow their instructions.

3. Do not pay the ransom

Paying the ransom does not guarantee that the files will be restored, and it encourages further attacks.

Stats on Ransomware

- The average cost of a ransomware attack is €4.15/$4.4 million. (Source: IBM Security)
- Ransomware attacks increased by 485% in 2020 compared to the previous year. (Source: Atlas VPN)
- The healthcare sector is the most targeted industry for ransomware attacks, followed by the manufacturing and construction sectors. (Source: Check Point Software)
- The average ransom demand in 2020 was €168,177/$178,254, an increase of 60% from the previous year. (Source: Coveware)
- The global damage from ransomware attacks is expected to reach €19/$20 billion by 2021. (Source: Cybersecurity Ventures)
- In a survey of 6,000 organisations, 51% reported experiencing a ransomware attack in the past year. (Source: Sophos)
- The cost of ransomware attacks is not limited to the ransom payment but also includes the cost of lost productivity, reputational damage, and data recovery. (Source: Cybersecurity Ventures)

Final thoughts on Ransomware

Ransomware attacks can have severe consequences for businesses, and employees play a crucial role in preventing and responding to such attacks. By adhering to these guidelines and staying aware of the risks, employees can help protect their organisations from ransomware attacks.

CHAPTER SIX

REMOTE WORKING

As more and more employees work remotely, cyber security has become an increasingly important concern. When working remotely, employees are often using their own devices and networks, which can pose a security risk.

Risks associated with working remotely

Hackers can use various tactics to gain access to an employee's computer or network, such as phishing emails, social engineering, or exploiting vulnerabilities in software.

As mentioned previously, one common tactic used by hackers is phishing, where they send an email that appears to be from a legitimate source, such as a bank or employer, and try to trick the recipient into clicking on a link or providing sensitive information. Social engineering is another tactic, where hackers use psychological manipulation to convince the recipient to divulge sensitive information or perform an action that compromises security.

Here are some tips for staying secure while working remotely:

1. **Use a secure network**

   Avoid using public Wi-Fi networks, which can be easily compromised. Ensure your home router has sufficient security controls such as authentication enabled.

2. **Keep software up to date**

   Ensure that all software, including operating systems, antivirus software, and web browsers, is kept up to date to prevent vulnerabilities from being exploited.

3. **Lock your devices**

   Even in safe locations such as home, it is vital to lock your devices when you are not using them.

4. **Use strong passwords**

   Use strong, unique passwords for each account, and consider using a password manager to generate and store passwords securely.

5. Be cautious of phishing emails

Be wary of unsolicited emails, especially those that ask for sensitive information or contain suspicious links or attachments.

6. Use two-factor authentication

When provided, enable two-factor authentication (2FA) on all accounts that support it. This adds a layer of security by requiring a code in addition to a password to access an account.

7. Personal and work separate

Separating work and personal activities on your device is important to protect sensitive work-related information. Use separate user accounts for personal and work-related activities, and avoid using work devices for personal use.

Stats on Remote Working and Security

- 91% of IT professionals surveyed by McAfee reported an increase in cyber threats due to remote work during the pandemic. (Source: McAfee)
- 60% of employees who work from home use personal devices for work purposes, increasing the risk of cyber-attacks. (Source: Tessian)
- In a survey of IT decision-makers, 57% said that remote workers pose a greater risk of phishing attacks. (Source: Mimecast)
- 45% of companies have experienced a security incident due to a remote worker. (Source: Bitglass)

- Only 35% of IT leaders believe that their organisation's security infrastructure is equipped to handle the rise in remote work. (Source: IBM)
- The average cost of a remote work-related security incident is €129,255/$137,000. (Source: OpenVPN)
- The most common security challenges associated with remote work are unsecured devices, VPN security, and employee security awareness. (Source: CrowdStrike)

Final thoughts on working from home

Cyber security is an important concern for remote workers, as they are often using their own devices and networks. By following these tips, remote workers can reduce the risk of being compromised by hackers and protect their sensitive information. As always, it's important to remain vigilant and aware of potential security threats and to report any suspicious activity to the appropriate authorities.

CHAPTER SEVEN

PHISHING

As an employee, you may receive numerous emails every day, some of which may be important while others may be spam or junk. Among the junk and spam, you may also come across a type of email known as "phishing" emails. Phishing is a type of cybercrime that involves sending fraudulent emails that appear to be from a legitimate source to trick you into providing sensitive information such as your login credentials or credit card details.

Phishing attacks are becoming increasingly common and sophisticated, and it is essential for employees to be aware of them and know how to recognise and avoid them. Here is a guide on what phishing is, how to recognise it, and what to do if you suspect a phishing attack.

What is phishing?

Phishing is a type of social engineering attack in which the attacker uses emails or messages to trick individuals into revealing sensitive information. The attackers often pose as a trusted entity such as a bank, government agency, or a company's IT department. The message may contain a link that takes you to a fake website that looks like the real one, where you are asked to enter your login credentials or other sensitive information.

Types of Phishing

Some popular Phishing examples that attackers are using are as follows:

- Phishing Email

  This is the most popular type of phishing. Most of the attacks are happening by email which usually contains a message to influence a potential victim to click a link or respond. The source of the message can look trustworthy; for example, the sender's email may look like that of a popular organisation. e.g., "orders@amazon.com" or an attacker can use the email "orders@amazom.com" which may look the same, but the spellings are different.

- Phishing Phone Call

  Another type of phishing is carried out via phone calls in which fraudsters make phone calls to people and try to trick them into giving sensitive information such as bank details or navigating them to a compromised website. The callers may make false promises and offer extraordinary items.

- ## Smishing & Vishing

    The mode of communication is a bit different from the above, but the format of the message and purpose is the same. In Smishing, the message is sent to the mobile phone as an SMS while in Vishing, a voice call is usually made. These messages may contain a Phishing link, threat, or any other message that may force the user to follow the sender.

- ## Spear Phishing

    This is a special kind of email phishing in which the attacker already knows some basic information about the user. E.g. Full Name, Residence, Phone Number, etc. This way, the credibility of the attacker becomes higher in the user's mind, and the user gets convinced more easily, resulting in a higher chance of a successful attack by an attacker.

- ## Whaling

    In this attack, a target is usually a high-profile person in an organisation. The attacker aims to harm the organisation somehow or to steal secret information, and the email may contain a malicious link or malware.

- ## Angler Phishing

    Angler Phishing is a relatively newer type of attack which uses social media applications. One example is how cybercriminals create fake accounts with the same logo as popular companies to commit fraud against that company's customers.

How to recognise phishing?

The attackers often use psychological tactics to create a sense of urgency or fear to convince you to take immediate action.

Phishing attacks can be challenging to spot, but here are some warning signs to look out for:

- An urgent or threatening tone

  Phishing emails often use a sense of urgency or fear to get you to act quickly. They may contain statements such as "Your account has been compromised, and you must act now."

- Unusual requests

  Be suspicious of emails that ask for unusual requests, such as sharing passwords or credit card details.

- Suspicious links

  Check the URLs of links before clicking on them. Attackers may use a domain name that looks like the real one, such as "bankofamerica.net" instead of "bankofamerica.com".

- Poor grammar or spelling mistakes

  Legitimate companies often proofread their emails before sending them. Phishing emails may contain poor grammar or spelling mistakes.

- Unusual sender email address

  The email address may contain an unusual combination of letters or numbers, or it may not match the domain name of the company the email claims to be from.

What to do if you suspect a phishing attack?

If you receive an email that you suspect is a phishing attack, here are some steps to take:

- Don't click on any links or download any attachments in the email.
- Report the email to your IT department or security team immediately.
- If you have already clicked on a link or entered any sensitive information, change your passwords immediately and notify your IT department or security team.
- Be vigilant in the future and report any suspicious emails or messages to your IT department or security team.

Stats on Phishing

Here are some statistics on phishing attacks:

- Phishing attacks account for 80% of reported security incidents. (Source: Verizon 2021 Data Breach Investigations Report)
- The global average cost of a phishing attack is $1.6 million. (Source: IBM 2020 Cost of a Data Breach Report)
- 1 in 3 targeted phishing emails results in a successful breach. (Source: Proofpoint 2020 State of the Phish Report)

- 96% of phishing attacks arrive via email. (Source: Cyber-security Ventures 2019 Official Annual Cybercrime Report)
- 66% of organisations experienced a phishing attack in 2020. (Source: CyberEdge 2020 Cyberthreat Defence Report)
- The top three industries targeted by phishing attacks are healthcare, manufacturing, and technology. (Source: KnowBe4 2020 Phishing by Industry Benchmarking Report)
- Phishing attacks are becoming more sophisticated, with 72% of phishing sites using HTTPS appearing more legitimate. (Source: Webroot 2020 Threat Report)

Final thoughts on Phishing

Phishing attacks are a growing threat to individuals and businesses alike. As an employee, it is essential to be aware of the warning signs and take steps to protect yourself and your organisation. Remember, if an email looks suspicious, it is always better to err on the side of caution and report it to your IT department or security team.

CHAPTER EIGHT

MOBILE DEVICES

Mobile devices have become an essential part of our lives. From personal communication to business operations, we rely heavily on mobile devices to stay connected and productive. However, this increased reliance on mobile devices has also brought about an increased risk of cyber threats, such as malware, phishing attacks, and data breaches.

Mobile device security awareness is critical for employees who use mobile devices for work-related tasks. A lack of attention can lead to security breaches that can compromise sensitive company information and put the organisation at risk.

Here are some important tips to keep in mind for mobile device security:

1. **Keep devices updated**

   Regular updates are essential for mobile devices to stay protected against new security threats. Employees should be encouraged to regularly update their mobile devices and apps to the latest versions when available or as per company policy.

2. **Password protection**

   Passwords are a basic security measure that should be used to protect mobile devices. Employees are advised to use strong passwords, change them regularly, and avoid using the same password across multiple accounts.

3. **Avoid public Wi-Fi**

   Public Wi-Fi networks are often unsecured and can be easily compromised. If available, employees should always use a virtual private network (VPN) when accessing company data or performing work-related tasks on their mobile devices.

4. **Be cautious of suspicious links**

   Phishing attacks are a common cyber threat, and they often come in the form of suspicious links or emails. Employees should be advised to avoid clicking on suspicious links or downloading attachments from unknown sources.

5. **Use company-approved apps**

Employees should only use company-approved apps for work-related tasks to minimise the risk of malware infections or data breaches. Avoid installing unauthorised apps or using personal accounts for company-related activities.

6. **Report suspicious activity**

Employees should be encouraged to report any suspicious activity or security breaches to their IT department or security team immediately. This can help to prevent further damage and minimise the impact of a security breach.

Stats on Mobile Devices and Security

- 83% of organisations allow their employees to use their personal mobile devices for work purposes. (Source: Bitglass)
- In a survey of IT decision-makers, 52% reported that mobile devices are the primary source of security breaches in their organisation. (Source: Check Point Software)
- 75% of mobile applications have at least one security vulnerability, according to a study by Positive Technologies. (Source: Positive Technologies)
- Android devices are more likely to be targeted by malware, with 98% of all mobile malware attacks targeting Android devices. (Source: Nokia)
- In a survey of IT professionals, 82% reported that they had experienced a mobile-related security incident in the past year. (Source: Dimensional Research)

- 65% of IT decision-makers believe that their organisation's security risk has increased due to the use of mobile devices. (Source: Check Point Software)
- The average cost of a mobile-related security incident is €2/$2.1 million. (Source: Ponemon Institute)

Final thoughts on Mobile Devices

Mobile device security awareness is crucial for employees who use mobile devices for work-related tasks. By practising good security habits, employees can help to keep their devices and sensitive company information safe from cyber threats.

CHAPTER NINE

SOCIAL ENGINEERING

Social engineering is a tactic used by cybercriminals to manipulate people into divulging sensitive information or performing actions that can compromise the security of an organisation. In a workplace setting, social engineering attacks can lead to data breaches, financial losses, and reputation damage. In this article, we will explore the importance of social engineering awareness for employees and provide tips on how to improve it.

Why is Social Engineering Awareness Important for Employees?

Social engineering attacks rely on human vulnerability and trust to succeed. Employees are often the first line of defence against these attacks, as they are the ones who handle sensitive information and have access to company systems. Here are some reasons why social engineering awareness is essential for employees:

- Preventing Data Breaches

  Social engineering attacks can lead to data breaches, which can be costly and damaging to a business. By being aware of social engineering tactics, employees can prevent cyber-criminals from gaining access to sensitive information.

- Protecting Financial Assets

  Social engineering attacks can also lead to financial losses, such as wire transfer fraud and invoice scams. By knowing how to identify and prevent these attacks, employees can protect the financial assets of the company.

- Maintaining Reputation

  A social engineering attack can damage the reputation of a business, as customers and partners may lose trust in the company's ability to protect their information. By preventing these attacks, employees can help maintain the reputation of the company.

Here are some examples of social engineering tactics used by cybercriminals:

- Phishing

  Phishing is a type of social engineering attack that involves sending fraudulent emails that appear to be from a legitimate source, such as a bank or an e-commerce website. The email may ask the recipient to click on a link or download an attachment that installs malware on their device or directs them to a fake website that collects their login credentials.

- Pretexting

  Pretexting is a type of social engineering attack that involves creating a false scenario to gain access to sensitive information. For example, a cybercriminal may pose as a customer service representative and ask for personal information such as a social security number or password.

- Baiting

  Baiting is a type of social engineering attack that involves offering something of value, such as a free USB drive, in exchange for the recipient's personal information or login credentials. The USB drive may contain malware that installs on the recipient's device and gives the cybercriminal access to their information.

- Tailgating

  Tailgating is a type of social engineering attack that involves following someone into a restricted area without proper authorisation. For example, a cybercriminal may wait for someone to enter a secure building and then follow them in without using an access card.

- Scareware

  Scareware is a type of social engineering attack that involves displaying a fake warning message on the recipient's device, claiming that their system has been infected with malware or a virus. The message may prompt the recipient to download software or click on a link that installs malware on their device.

Stats on Social Engineering

- Social engineering attacks account for 98% of all cyber-attacks. (Source: Check Point Software)
- Phishing attacks are the most common form of social engineering, with 94% of malware being delivered via email. (Source: Verizon 2021 Data Breach Investigations Report)
- In a survey of IT decision-makers, 88% reported that their organisation had experienced a social engineering attack in the past year. (Source: Mimecast)
- The most common targets of social engineering attacks are employees, followed by customers and third-party vendors. (Source: KnowBe4)
- The average cost of a social engineering attack is €1.4/$1.5 million. (Source: Check Point Software)
- Social media platforms are increasingly being used in social engineering attacks, with 66% of social media-related incidents involving phishing. (Source: Proofpoint)

- The most common types of information targeted in social engineering attacks are login credentials, personal information, and financial information. (Source: Mimecast)

Final thoughts on Social Engineering

Social engineering awareness is essential for preventing cyber-attacks and protecting the security of a business. It's important to be aware of these tactics and to take steps to protect yourself and your organisation from these types of attacks.

CHAPTER TEN

CLEAN DESK

Maintaining a clean desk is not only important for an employee's productivity and well-being, but it's also a crucial aspect of security. In this article, we'll explore the connection between a clean desk and security awareness and offer tips for employees to keep their workspace secure.

Why is a clean desk important for security awareness?

- Protects sensitive information

    Sensitive information such as passwords, confidential documents, and personal data should never be left lying around on a desk. A clean desk policy ensures that employees secure their sensitive information when not in use, which reduces the risk of data breaches and identity theft.

- Prevents unauthorised access

    Leaving a computer unlocked or documents on a desk can allow unauthorised access to sensitive information. A clean desk policy encourages employees to lock their computer screens and secure their documents when not in use, which reduces the risk of unauthorised access.

- Promotes compliance

  Certain industries and organisations require compliance with strict regulations and standards, such as HIPAA in the healthcare industry or GDPR in the EU. A clean desk policy can help ensure compliance with these regulations by keeping sensitive information secure and confidential.

Tips for maintaining a clean and secure desk

- Secure sensitive information

  Sensitive information should be secured when not in use. This could include paper notes with sensitive information on them and locking documents in a filing cabinet.

- Follow the clean desk policy

  Organisations may have a clean desk policy in place that outlines the requirements for maintaining a secure workspace. Employees should familiarise themselves with this policy and follow it to ensure compliance and reduce security risks.

- Dispose of documents properly

  Documents containing sensitive information should be disposed of properly. This could include shredding them before disposing of them in a secure bin.

- Report any suspicious activity

  Employees should be aware of their surroundings and report any suspicious activity or individuals to their security team or manager. This could include noticing someone attempting to access their computer or documents without permission.

Stats on Clean Desk

- In a study of office workers, 71% admitted to leaving sensitive documents on their desks overnight. (Source: Fellowes)
- A survey of IT professionals found that 44% of data breaches are caused by employee mistakes, such as leaving sensitive information on an unsecured desk. (Source: Shred-It)
- A clean desk policy can reduce the risk of information being stolen or compromised in the event of a break-in or theft. (Source: CSO Online)
- A clean desk policy can also help to improve employee awareness of security risks and reinforce the importance of security best practices. (Source: Security Magazine)
- In a study of office workers, 71% said that they would be more likely to follow a clean desk policy if it was enforced by their manager. (Source: Fellowes)
- The use of a clean desk policy can also help organisations comply with regulations such as the Health Insurance Portability and Accountability Act (HIPAA) and the General Data Protection Regulation (GDPR). (Source: Information Security Buzz)

Final thoughts on a clean desk

A clean desk policy is a crucial aspect of security awareness for employees. By protecting sensitive information, preventing unauthorised access, and promoting compliance, a clean desk can help reduce security risks and keep the organisation secure. Following these tips can help employees maintain a clean and secure workspace, and contribute to the overall security of the organisation.

CHAPTER ELEVEN

INCIDENT REPORTING & RESPONSE

Even with the best security practices in place, it is still possible for cyber security incidents to occur. Employees must understand the importance of incident reporting and the steps to take when they suspect a security breach or other cyber threat.

Best practices for incident reporting and response:

- Recognize the signs of a security incident

  Be aware of the signs that may indicate a security breach, such as unusual system activity, unauthorised access attempts, or unexpected data loss.

- Follow company procedures

  Familiarise yourself with your organisation's incident reporting and response procedures. Know whom to contact and the steps to take if you suspect a security incident.

- **Report incidents immediately**

  If you suspect a security breach or other cyber security incident, report it immediately to your IT department or designated security contact. Prompt reporting can help mitigate the damage and enable a faster response to the threat.

- **Preserve evidence**

  If you discover a security incident, avoid altering or deleting any relevant data or system logs, as this information may be crucial for investigating the incident.

- **Participate in incident response training**

  Attend any training sessions or workshops offered by your organisation on incident response to better understand your role in the process and improve your ability to respond effectively to security incidents.

- **Learn from incidents**

  After an incident has been resolved, review the lessons learned and use this information to improve your security practices and prevent future incidents.

- **Communicate with your team**

  Keep your team members informed of any security incidents and the steps taken to address them. Open communication can help create a culture of security awareness and promote a proactive approach to cyber security.

Stat on Incident Reporting and Response

- According to a survey conducted by the Ponemon Institute, only 29% of employees report potential security incidents to their IT department, meaning that the majority of incidents go unreported (Source: Ponemon Institute's 2021 State of Password and Authentication Security Behaviours Report).
- The average time to detect a data breach is 207 days, and the average time to contain a data breach is 73 days, emphasising the importance of timely incident reporting and response (Source: IBM Security's 2021 Cost of a Data Breach Report).
- 90% of data breaches can be prevented with basic security hygiene, including incident reporting and response (Source: Verizon's 2021 Data Breach Investigations Report).
- In a survey of IT and security professionals, 44% stated that they have encountered challenges with employees failing to report potential security incidents, highlighting the need for better education and awareness (Source: Help Net Security's 2021 Cybersecurity Report).
- Effective incident response can reduce the cost of a data breach by an average of €1.9/$2 million (Source: IBM Security's 2021 Cost of a Data Breach Report).

Final thoughts on Incident Reporting and Response

By adapting these best practices for incident reporting and response, employees can play a critical role in detecting and addressing security threats, minimising the impact of cyber security incidents, and helping to maintain a secure work environment.

CHAPTER TWELVE

CONCLUSION

In today's digital age, cyber security awareness is critical for organisations to protect their digital assets and maintain a secure work environment. By educating employees on best practices for password management, VPN usage, phishing awareness, and email security, organisations can minimise their risk of cyber-attacks and data breaches. Employees play a critical role in maintaining a secure work environment, making ongoing cyber security education and awareness a top priority for all organisations.

It is also important for organisations to regularly review and update their security policies, procedures, and training programs to ensure that they remain effective and relevant in the face of evolving threats. By taking a proactive approach to cyber security, organisations can better protect their digital assets and reduce the risk of cyber-attacks and data breaches.

In conclusion, cyber security is a shared responsibility that requires collaboration and vigilance from all employees within an organisation. By working together and prioritising cyber security awareness, organisations can create a culture of security and reduce the risk of cyber threats.

Printed in Great Britain
by Amazon

21670513R00034